Is your business on the rig
your life? How can you and
awesome?

A really great question can change your life. Join us on a Mind Hike, a journey to help you illuminate your business path and make the right choices for you.

Mind Hike is a series of 365 targeted questions in a journal format for business owners and other leaders. This is a two-way journey. After you complete the initial questions, you will revisit each one a second time to see how you, your life and your business have changed over time. Your Mind Hike journey will get you thinking about what is important to you, what is working in your business, and ultimately, what will bring you joy, success and satisfaction.

This guided Mind Hike journey will help you:

* Be intentional about the choices that you make.
* Be clear about your goals and your priorities.
* Think through your relationships and how (or if) to move forward.
* Develop a plan for the future.

Embark with us on Mind Hike to plumb the depths of your mind and find the answers that are hidden deep inside. Life (and business) can be a treacherous journey — let Mind Hike be the guide.

Legal Stuff

You got this, dude!

www.mindhikejourney.com

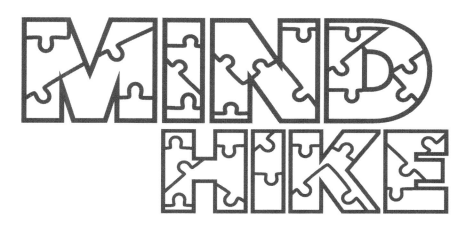

A 365 question journey of self-discovery

BUSINESS EDITION

ABOUT US

ELISSA:

Elissa's grandpa always swore that "Safer" (Elissa's maiden name) meant "horse thief", and that Elissa came from a long line of horse thieves. However, Elissa has yet to steal a horse.

In her day job (as a franchise and business lawyer), Elissa has helped hundreds of people start their own businesses. Outside of work, Elissa swam with sharks in the South Pacific, hiked from border to border in Israel, backpacked through mainland China and is always up for a new adventure.

In recent years, Elissa's adventures have taken a quieter and more harrowing turn–Elissa has become a mom and has also turned her journey inward. Elissa has become an enthusiastic (and unskilled) meditator and an aficionado of anything that has "personal growth" in the title.

MIKE

Dad. Husband. Lawyer. Entrepreneur.
Beer drinker. Look, there's a squirrel.

Welcome to Mind Hike

WHAT IS A MIND HIKE?
(DICTIONARY VERSION)

MIND: the element of a person that enables them to be aware of the world and their experiences, to think, and to feel; the faculty of consciousness and thought.

HIKE: to walk or march a great distance, especially through rural areas, for pleasure, exercise, military training, or the like.

WHAT IS A MIND HIKE?
(OUR VERSION)

For the past few years, we have been on our own journey of self-improvement through journaling, reading and meditation. We wrote this journal in the middle of a global pandemic. We each have adventures we wish we could embark on. Elissa had hoped to spend time exploring the world. Mike had plans to visit as many beer festivals as possible (or at the very least to spend a few days outside of Colorado). These big plans didn't turn out so well. So, we turned to explorations within our own selves. And Mind Hike (Mike's baby) was born.

Mind Hike, therefore, (we promise this is the only legalese in this book) for us is a personal odyssey. It is a time and place for self-exploration, self-understanding and self-improvement. We hope that you enjoy taking the mind hike as much as we have creating it.

Why Questions?

We've all heard the same phrase for years: "There is no such thing as a stupid question." And some of you may have also heard the related: "Of course there are stupid questions.... And your question was a really stupid question." OK, I may have actually heard that second phrase from my boss (co-author), Mike (Hi, Mike).

While this age-long debate will continue, we believe that a really great question can change your life. (We can't help it, we're both lawyers.) We want to help you illuminate your choices and your path. We hope you enjoy your journey!

How to use this Book

 Spend as much or as little time as you want.

 Do a question a day. 2 a day. 45 a day. Whatever. It's your hike; so your pace.

 Make sure to make this a round-trip journey and answer each question at two separate times. It's important to see how your answers and your day-to-day experiences change over time.

 We had originally imagined this journey as a day-by-day exploration (like a daily multi-year journal). But we realized that these questions really should be your own. Do you have a free afternoon? You could complete the first leg of the journey all in one day. Do you feel like answering 10 questions in one sitting? Go for it. Are you at a company retreat? Responding to the Mind Hike questions would be a great weekend activity.

FAQ

(we've tried to answer a few
of your non-stupid questions)

? Do I need to start my journal on a certain day? [We already answered this. Read the intro.]

? Do I need to complete one question each day? [Same here. See above.]

? Can I use one word answers? Yes. (See what we did there?) As you can see in our samples, Mike tends to answer quickly in one word answers and Elissa prefers to pontificate (much to her children's dismay). Answer in whatever way is helpful for you.

? What if the questions don't apply for/to me? We wrote this journal with business owners and leaders in mind. We're sure you've all played the fortune-cookie game (i.e., add "with a partner" to the end of each fortune — haha, endless amusement). Add or change these questions in any way that is helpful to you, in the same manner.

? What if I don't have an answer? : We think not having an answer is actually very instructive. If you don't have an answer, (especially on both rounds of answering) spend some time thinking about why you didn't have an answer. Is it just a question that is irrelevant to your business? Or is it an area that you don't think about enough? Is it something you avoid thinking about?

MIND HIKE

? <u>How many questions are there really?</u> 365 if you do it once, 730 if you do it twice. And more if you do bonus questions (we didn't feel like doing the math for the bonus questions but more than 730 for sure). The arrow pointing to the right is for the first round of answers. The arrow pointing to the left is for the second go around.

? <u>What should I do with my answers?</u> Our favorite part of these inner journeys is actually trying to get out of our own heads (occupational hazard for anyone who spends a lot of time by themselves at their computer). We like to think about it as blunt honesty: you peer inside, scoop it out, and then look at it all with clear eyes. "It" being all those dreams and all the angst that we all have clogging up our brains. Once you have it all out in the open, you may want to handle the next steps alone. Or you may want to enlist a friend. We urge you to look for patterns and "a-ha" moments. Has anything changed in your second go-around with the questions? What have you been focusing on? What is holding you back? (Ah, an answer with more questions.)
Finally, we encourage you to join us on our Mind Hike blog (www.mindhikejourney.com) and join other adventurers who are also on this journey. We hope we can all provide guidance and support for each other.

? <u>What should I do in the Free Space?</u> You can do anything you want with the Free Space space. Hence the name, Free Space. (Darn. We used legalese again. Sorry about that.) You can list gratitude points, draw doodles, further elaborate on the question... seriously. Anything you want. In our ideal world, you will have a life-changing epiphany that you might write down (inspired of course, by a brilliant

question you've just answered). But you can use it to jot down your grocery list or just doodle, if that's your preference.

? <u>Tell me about the Bonus Questions.</u> This is not even a question. #FAQFAIL. The bonus questions are additional questions (bonus) that go deeper into a topic or take a question in a different direction. Feel free to answer them, ignore them or turn them into Free Space (see Free Space FAQ above).

? <u>What's all this about a round-trip journey?</u> Glad you asked! We all want to go somewhere, but we've got to return home eventually. The idea behind Mind Hike is to take your journey by answering 365 questions, and revisiting those same questions to figure out what you've learned on your travels.

MIND HIKE

MIKE'S SAMPLE

QUESTION 15

What was your most recent great idea?

➡️ write a book.   Date 10/1/20

(bucket list item)

(fun experience)

(learn process)

⬅️ Write a sequel   Date 10/1/21
to the book

(continue above points)

(fun)

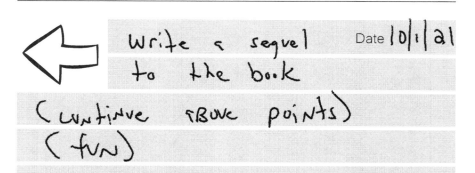

Free Space

Ideas

Write follow up book

start blog

To Do: Fix Computer issue

MIND HIKE

ELISSA'S SAMPLE

QUESTION 17

What item has been on your to-do list the longest?

Date 3|18|19

Reviewing resumes and responding to job candidates. Yuck

Date 8|5|19

Responding to those job candidates! Just kidding. Choosing a college counselor for Sam :-)

Free Space ooh. Deep thought (although probably obvious to anyone else). I'm avoiding any task that I feel emotional about. Like - deciding to hire someone now or next year. And sending my baby to college :-)

MIND HIKE

ACKNOWLEDGEMENTS

Mike

I would like to thank Brenda, Eli, Emma and Pierce (Jackson). You make life fun. I would also like to thank my baby sister Tracy Weldon for supporting me and inspiring me to be a better person. I would also like to thank Jeffrey Stuffings. You are the best book club member a person could ask for. And finally, Mom. Thanks for always saying that I am your favorite (even though we know Tracy is).

Elissa

I dedicate this book to all my favorite people in the world: Steve, Sam, Lily, my parents, my favorite brother and the friends that share my days. You make everything better.

WELCOME
TO YOUR JOURNEY

QUESTION 1

Are you happy?

→ Date

_____

_____

_____

_____

← Date

Free Space

MIND HIKE

QUESTION 2

What keeps you awake at night?

Date

Date

Free Space

QUESTION 3

How do you define success?

Date

Date

Free Space

MIND HIKE

QUESTION 4

What is your highest and best purpose?

Date

Date

Free Space

MIND HIKE

QUESTION 5

Who is the company's biggest
champion (employee)?

Date
_____

_____

_____

_____

Date

Bonus Question: **Nonemployee?**

MIND HIKE

QUESTION 6

What is your best hidden skill?

Date

_____

_____

_____

_____

Date

Bonus Question: How often do you use this skill?

MIND HIKE

QUESTION 7

What could make you walk away from your position today?

Date

Date

Free Space

MIND HIKE

QUESTION 8

When was the last time you crossed the line?

Date

Date

Free Space

QUESTION 9

If you got hit by a bus tomorrow, who would take over your role?

Date

Date

Free Space

MIND HIKE

QUESTION 10

What has been the best year of your life?

Date

_____

_____

_____

_____

Date

Bonus Question: **The worst year?**

MIND HIKE

QUESTION 11

What is your least favorite work task?

Date
_____

_____

_____

_____

_____

Date

Bonus Question: **Favorite?**

MIND HIKE

QUESTION 12

If your company was a food,
what food would it be?

Date

Date

Bonus Question: Dessert?

MIND HIKE

Are you more liked in your family or at your job?

Date

Date

Free Space

MIND HIKE

QUESTION 14

If you had to fire one client today (or discontinue one product), who (what) would it be?

Date
_____

_____

_____

_____

Date

Free Space

MIND HIKE

QUESTION 15

What was your most recent great idea?

Date

Date

Free Space

QUESTION 16

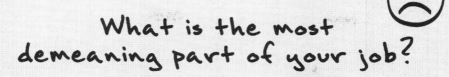

What is the most
demeaning part of your job?

Date

Date

Bonus Question: **Rewarding?**

MIND HIKE

What item has been on your to-do list the longest?

Date

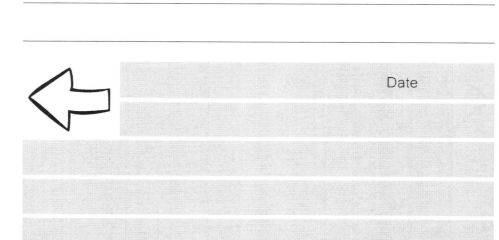

Date

Free Space

QUESTION 18

When was the last time you were the bottleneck?

Date

_____

_____

_____

_____

Date

Free Space

MIND HIKE

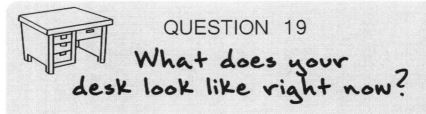

QUESTION 19

What does your desk look like right now?

Date
_____

_____

_____

_____

Date

Free Space

MIND HIKE

QUESTION 20

How dependent is your company on a healthy economy?

➡️ _____ Date

_____

_____

_____

_____

⬅️ Date

Bonus Question: How can you be more independent?

MIND HIKE

QUESTION 21

Behind every great leader is_____ (fill in the blank)

Date

Date

Free Space

QUESTION 22

If you were granted one wish for your company, what would it be? (You can't wish for more wishes.)

Date

Date

Bonus Question: **2 wishes?**

MIND HIKE

QUESTION 23

If you could add any new product or service today, what would it be?

Date

Date

Free Space

MIND HIKE

QUESTION 24

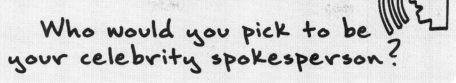

Who would you pick to be your celebrity spokesperson?

Date
_____

_____

_____

_____

Date
_____

_____

_____

_____

Free Space

MIND HIKE

QUESTION 25

Who was the last person you made prove themselves to you?

Date

Date

Bonus Question: **Why?**

QUESTION 26

What is your "secret sauce"?

Date

Date

Free Space

QUESTION 27

"Keep It Simple, Stupid." How much do you agree or disagree with this?

Date
_____

Date

Free Space

MIND HIKE

QUESTION 28

How supportive is your significant other of your career?

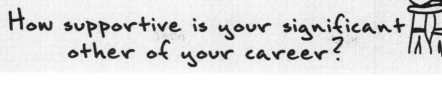

Date
_____

_____

_____

_____

Date

Tip: (If no significant other —
substitute best friend or parent)

MIND HIKE

QUESTION 29

What was the last thing you cleared from your search history?

Date

Date

Free Space

MIND HIKE

QUESTION 30

If you had to trade positions with one person in your company, who would it be?

Date

Date

Free Space

MIND HIKE

QUESTION 31

Which customers / clients / partners share your values?

→ Date
_____

← Date

Bonus Question: **Which do not?**

MIND HIKE

QUESTION 32

What is the best compliment you've recently received?

Date

Date

Bonus Question: Recently given?

MIND HIKE

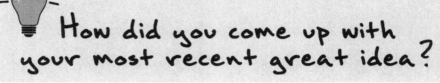

QUESTION 33

How did you come up with your most recent great idea?

Date
_____

_____

_____

_____

Date

Free Space

MIND HIKE

QUESTION 34

You just found out that the company is going bankrupt next week. What do you do next?

Date
_____

Date

Bonus Question: What if the company were going bankrupt next year?

MIND HIKE

QUESTION 35

1 Describe your company in one word.

⇒ _____ Date

_____

_____

_____

⇐ _____ Date

Bonus Question: **Describe yourself using one word.**

MIND HIKE

QUESTION 36

"Can't see the forest for the trees."
How have you focused on the forest?

Date

Date

Bonus Question: The trees?

MIND HIKE

QUESTION 37

Why do businesses fail?

→ _____ Date

_____

_____

_____

← _____ Date

Free Space

MIND HIKE

QUESTION 38

What company technology do you hate the most?

Date
_____

_____

_____

_____

Date

Bonus Question: **Like the most?**

MIND HIKE

QUESTION 39

How can you make your company more nimble?

Date

_____

_____

_____

_____

Date

Tip: Nimble means quick and light in movement or action; agile.

MIND HIKE

How connected is your company to your community?

Date
_____

_____

_____

_____

Date

Bonus Question: What is your community?

QUESTION 41

"Hope for the best and plan for the worst." When was the last time you followed this advice?

Date

Date

Free Space

MIND HIKE

QUESTION 42

What are the biggest threats to your company?

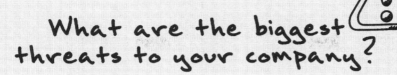

Date
_____

Date

Free Space

QUESTION 43

How much more profitable do you expect to be next year?

Date

Date

Free Space

MIND HIKE

QUESTION 44

What is your reputation in your industry?

Date

Date

Bonus Question: Who has a better reputation?

MIND HIKE

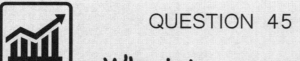

QUESTION 45

What is your most recent sales success story?

Date

Date

Bonus Question: Sales failure?

MIND HIKE

QUESTION 46

What is your current exit plan?

Date

Date

Free Space

MIND HIKE

What is your elevator pitch?

Date

Date

Tip: An "elevator pitch" is a short sales pitch.

MIND HIKE

QUESTION 48

If you were to relocate your corporate office anywhere, where would it be?

Date
_____

Date

Free Space

MIND HIKE

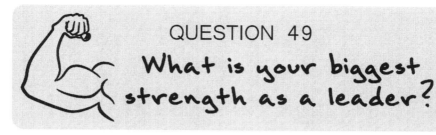

QUESTION 49

What is your biggest strength as a leader?

Date

Date

Bonus Question: Your second biggest strength?

MIND HIKE

QUESTION 50

What is your go-to song to get work done?

Date

Date

Free Space

The hardest part of the journey is taking the first step.

GUIDEPOST #1: Well, here you are. You made it this far. Take a load off. There are beers (or water, if that's more your style) on the table.

If you have reached this point, we can only assume that you have made it through this first leg of your journey. Or you've skipped over all of the first set of questions, and landed here anyhow (which is also fine, this is your journey). In either event, welcome! We're happy to see you.

Let's celebrate your ascent through this first part of the journey. Go find someone among your people and spend an hour together. You can be moving or eating or even zooming. Just spend this time together.

TASK: Share 5 questions from your Mind Hike journey with a friend, colleague, mentor or a stranger. Then chat about the questions, the answers and life.

QUESTION 51

Would you be a customer/ client of your company?

Date

Date

Bonus Question: **Why or why not?**

MIND HIKE

$ Do you look at the financials
for your business as much as you should?

Date

Date

Free Space

MIND HIKE

QUESTION 53

If someone offered you $1,000,000, would you sell your business?

Date
_____

Date

Bonus Question: If you don't own the business, is it worth $1,000,000? Why/Why not?

MIND HIKE

QUESTION 54

If you had to divest one area of your business, what would it be?

Date
_____

Date

Tip: To "divest" means to reduce for financial, ethical or political reasons; or sell an existing business.

QUESTION 55

When was the last time you were willing to change?

Date
_____

_____

_____

_____

Date
_____

_____

_____

_____

Bonus Question: **Unwilling?**

MIND HIKE

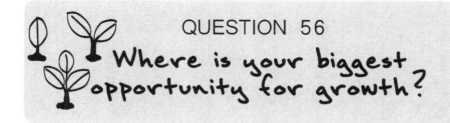

QUESTION 56

Where is your biggest opportunity for growth?

Date

_____

Date

Free Space

MIND HIKE

QUESTION 57

When were you last terminated (as an employee or as a provider)?

Date

Date

Bonus Question: **Why?**

MIND HIKE

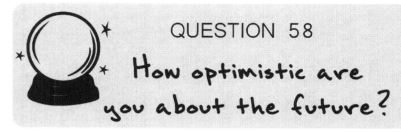

QUESTION 58

How optimistic are you about the future?

Date

Date

Free Space

MIND HIKE

QUESTION 59

When was the last time you were criticized?

Date
_____

Date

Bonus Question: You criticized someone else?

MIND HIKE

QUESTION 60

What was the last performance review you were involved in?

Date

Date

Free Space

MIND HIKE

QUESTION 61

If you received a $100,000 investment to spend on the business, how would you spend it?

Date
_____

Date

Free Space

QUESTION 62

What was the last networking event that you attended?

Date
_____

_____

_____

_____

Date

Bonus Question: **Was it worthwhile?**

QUESTION 63

What's your signature move?

Date

Date

Free Space

MIND HIKE

QUESTION 64

What skill would you like to acquire?

→ Date
_____

_____

_____

_____

← Date

Free Space

QUESTION 65

Do you spend the right amount of time at work?

Date

Date

Bonus Question: How would your family (or friends) answer this question?

MIND HIKE

QUESTION 66

Who is your biggest flight risk?

→ Date
_____

_____

_____

_____

← Date

Free Space

QUESTION 67

When was the last time you turned down new business?

Date
_____

Date

Free Space

MIND HIKE

QUESTION 68

When was the last time you paid-to-play?

Date
_____

Date

Tip: **For example, have you paid for the privilege of speaking at a conference?**

QUESTION 69

If you picked a movie to motivate your team, what movie would it be?

Date

Date

Free Space

MIND HIKE

QUESTION 70

What was the most productive thing you've done recently?

Date

Date

Free Space

MIND HIKE

QUESTION 71

Who would you hire if you had
to rehire one former employee?

Date

Date

Free Space

MIND HIKE

QUESTION 72

Does your role allow you to be true to yourself?

Date

Date

Free Space

MIND HIKE

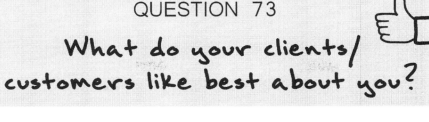

What do your clients/customers like best about you?

Date
_____

_____

_____

_____

Date

Bonus Question: **Dislike?**

MIND HIKE

QUESTION 74

In what other field could you be successful?

Free Space

MIND HIKE

QUESTION 75

$

What is (or will be) the largest single item in your budget?

Date

←

Date

Free Space

MIND HIKE

QUESTION 76

When was the last time you were stabbed in the front?

Date
_____

_____

_____

_____

_____

Date

"True friends stab you in the front." - Oscar Wilde

QUESTION 77

Who is your favorite person today?

Date

Date

Free Space

MIND HIKE

QUESTION 78

What is your biggest distraction?

→ _____ Date

_____

_____

_____

← Date

Free Space

MIND HIKE

QUESTION 79

Who was the last co-worker to annoy you?

Date

Date

Bonus Question: To make you smile?

MIND HIKE

QUESTION 80

When was the last time you ruined someone's day?

Date

Date

Free Space

MIND HIKE

QUESTION 81

What is one thing you can do to improve your productivity?

Date

Date

Bonus Question: **Worsen?**

MIND HIKE

QUESTION 82

How are you different today, than you were one year ago?

Date

_____

_____

_____

_____

Date

Bonus Question: 10 years ago?

MIND HIKE

QUESTION 83

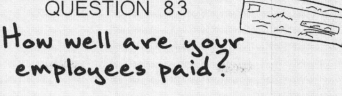

How well are your employees paid?

Date

_____

Date

Bonus Question: **What is the best benefit your company offers?**

MIND HIKE

QUESTION 84

What 21st-century skills are you lacking?

Date
_____

Date

Free Space

QUESTION 85

Who could/ should you mentor?

Date

Date

Free Space

QUESTION 86

You are restarting your company and can only keep one employee. Who do you keep?

Date

Date

Free Space

MIND HIKE

What was the last stupid thing you did at work?

Date

Date

Bonus Question: **Smart thing?**

MIND HIKE

QUESTION 88

What is the most difficult part of your job?

Date

Date

Bonus Question: **Easiest part?**

QUESTION 89

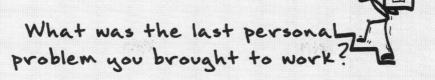

What was the last personal problem you brought to work?

Date
_____

Date

Bonus Question: **Last business problem you brought home?**

MIND HIKE

QUESTION 90

When was the last time you were a "straight shooter"?

Date

Date

Free Space

MIND HIKE

QUESTION 91

What advice would you have for someone who was entering your field (or wanted your position)?

Date

Date

Free Space

MIND HIKE

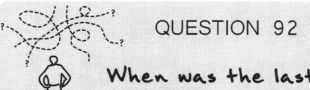

QUESTION 92

When was the last time
you second-guessed yourself?

Date

Date

Free Space

MIND HIKE

QUESTION 93

What is your biggest hiring regret?

Date

Date

Free Space

QUESTION 94

Who is the most street smart person in your company?

→ Date
_____

_____

_____

_____

← Date

Bonus Question: Book smart?

MIND HIKE

QUESTION 95

What is the most embarrassing thing you've done at work?

Date

Date

Free Space

QUESTION 96

Grammar be hard. What grammar mistakes drive you crazy?

Date

Date

Free Space

QUESTION 97

How often do you really listen?

Date

Date

Free Space

MIND HIKE

What isn't working
at your company?

Date

Date

Free Space

MIND HIKE

QUESTION 99

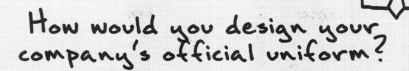

How would you design your company's official uniform?

Date

Date

Free Space

MIND HIKE

QUESTION 100

Is it too late to start over?

→ _____ Date

_____

_____

_____

_____

← _____ Date

Free Space

MIND HIKE

QUESTION 101

What is one of your strengths that is also a weakness?

Date
_____

Date

Free Space

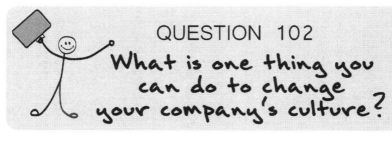

QUESTION 102

What is one thing you can do to change your company's culture?

→ Date
_____

_____

_____

_____

← Date

Free Space

QUESTION 103

What have you put off doing?

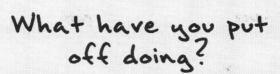

Date
_____

_____

_____

_____

Date

Free Space

MIND HIKE

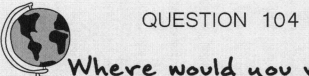

QUESTION 104

Where would you rather be right now?

Date

Date

Free Space

MIND HIKE

QUESTION 105

What is your biggest firing regret?

Date

Date

Free Space

MIND HIKE

When was the last time you were inconsistent?

Date

_____

Date

Free Space

MIND HIKE

QUESTION 107

Things happen for a reason. Can you give one recent example?

Date

Date

Free Space

MIND HIKE

What was the last task that you delegated?

Date

Date

Free Space

MIND HIKE

QUESTION 109

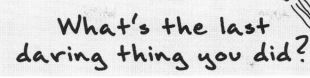

What's the last daring thing you did?

Date

Date

Free Space

MIND HIKE

QUESTION 110

Which co-workers most share your values?

Date

_____

_____

_____

_____

Date

Bonus Question: **Which do not?**

QUESTION 111

Would you be willing to work for someone else?

Date

Date

Bonus Question: **Why or why not?**

MIND HIKE

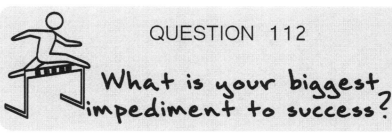

QUESTION 112

What is your biggest impediment to success?

Date

Date

Free Space

QUESTION 113

How well are you able to leave work behind when the work day ends?

→

Date
_____

_____

_____

_____

←

Date

Free Space

MIND HIKE

QUESTION 114

What are you doing to keep up with the changes in the world?

Date

Date

Free Space

MIND HIKE

QUESTION 115

Describe your ideal work environment.

Date
_____

_____

_____

_____

Date
_____

Bonus Question: What is your actual work environment?

QUESTION 116

When was the last time you were really challenged?

Date

Date

Free Space

MIND HIKE

QUESTION 117

What's your most recent missed opportunity?

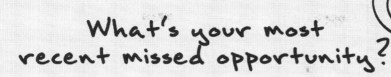

Date

_____

Date

Free Space

MIND HIKE

QUESTION 118

What are you neglecting right now?

Date

Date

Bonus Question: **Why?**

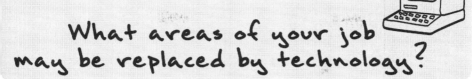

QUESTION 119

What areas of your job may be replaced by technology?

Date
_____

_____

_____

_____

Date

Free Space

MIND HIKE

QUESTION 120

What are your biggest weaknesses as a leader?

Date

_____

Date

Bonus Question: How can you improve them?

MIND HIKE

QUESTION 121

When was your last all company meeting?

Date

Date

Free Space

MIND HIKE

QUESTION 122

When was the last time you were angry with a co-worker?

Date

Date

Free Space

QUESTION 123

" **"**

What's your favorite quote?

➡️ Date
_____

⬅️ Date

Free Space

MIND HIKE

QUESTION 124

What failures have shaped who you are?

Date _____

_____

_____

_____

_____

Date

Bonus Question: **What successes?**

QUESTION 125

Rank the following from most to least important: wealth, power, fame, satisfaction, work-life balance, improving the world.

Date
_____

_____

_____

_____

Date

Free Space

MIND HIKE

QUESTION 126

What is your favorite thing in your office?

Date

Date

Bonus Question: Least favorite thing?

QUESTION 127

What changes need to be made in your industry?

Date _____

_____

_____

_____

_____

Date

Bonus Question: **What is preventing them?**

MIND HIKE

QUESTION 128

What was your last successful negotiation?

Date

Date

Bonus Question: Failed negotiation?

QUESTION 129

When was the last time you celebrated?

Date

Date

Free Space

MIND HIKE

QUESTION 130

How much energy do you spend worrying about being liked by your co-workers?

→ _____ Date

←

Date

Bonus Question: **Respected?**

QUESTION 131

What is one thing you can do to handle stress better?

Date

Date

Free Space

MIND HIKE

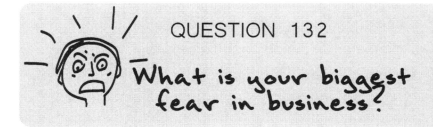

QUESTION 132

What is your biggest fear in business?

Date

_____

Date

Bonus Question: Do your co-workers share this fear?

QUESTION 133

Which co-worker do you have the least contact with?

Date
_____

Date

Bonus Question: **Why?**

MIND HIKE

QUESTION 134

What is one thing you can change to be 10% happier?

Date

Date

Free Space

MIND HIKE

QUESTION 135

Who would be better in your role than you?

Date
_____

_____

_____

_____

Date

Free Space

MIND HIKE

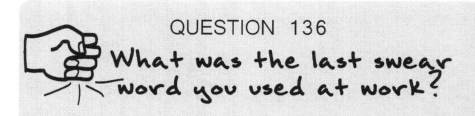

QUESTION 136

What was the last swear word you used at work?

Date
_____

Date

Bonus Question: **Who did you say it to?**

QUESTION 137

You are setting up the new office layout. Who gets the office next to yours?

Date
_____

Date

Bonus Question: **The office farthest away?**

MIND HIKE

QUESTION 138

When was the last time you were really shocked?

Date

Date

Free Space

MIND HIKE

What are you suffering from right now?

Date
_____

_____

_____

_____

Date

"Suffering usually relates to wanting things to be different than the way they are." - Pema Chodron

MIND HIKE

QUESTION 140

How do you dress your part?

→ Date
_____

_____

_____

_____

← Date

Free Space

QUESTION 141

If you could hire anyone in the world, who would it be?

Date

Date

Free Space

MIND HIKE

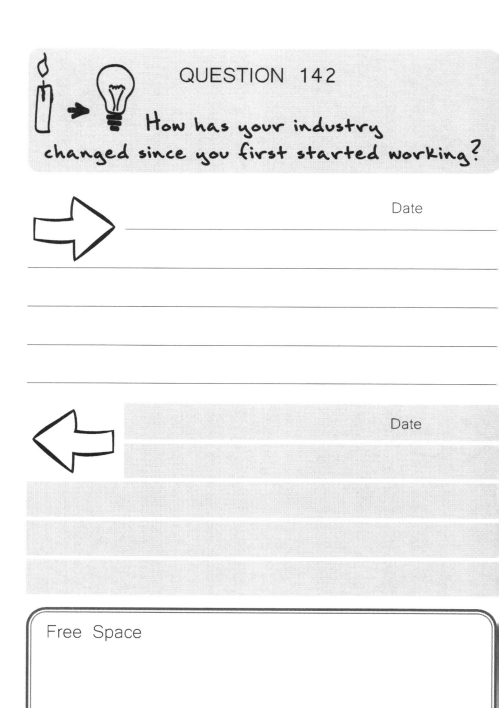

QUESTION 142

How has your industry changed since you first started working?

Date

Date

Free Space

QUESTION 143

When was the last time you dealt with an exception-not-the-rule situation?

Date

Date

Free Space

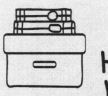

QUESTION 144

How can you become better organized?

Date

_____

Date

Free Space

QUESTION 145

Would you rather have more money or more free time?

Date
_____

Date

Free Space

MIND HIKE

QUESTION 146

What fictional company best describes your company's culture?

Date
_____

_____

_____

_____

Date

Free Space

MIND HIKE

QUESTION 147

Who is your mentor?

Date
_____

_____

_____

_____

Date

Bonus Question: If you could pick any mentor, who would you pick?

MIND HIKE

QUESTION 148

How much do you value loyalty?

→ Date
_____

_____

_____

_____

_____

← Date

Free Space

MIND HIKE

QUESTION 149

How old do you feel today?

Date
_____

_____

_____

_____

Date

Free Space

MIND HIKE

What was the last system change that you implemented?

Date
_____

Date

Bonus Question: **Was it successful?**

MIND HIKE

QUESTION 151

What is the perfect workday?

Date

Date

Free Space

QUESTION 152

If you had the chance to re-do your hiring choices, which of your current team would make the cut?

Date

Date

Free Space

MIND HIKE

What do you want to be an expert in?

Date
_____

_____

_____

_____

Date

Bonus Question: **What are you an expert in?**

MIND HIKE

QUESTION 154

What is the best thing
a former boss would
say about you?

Date

_____

Date

Bonus Question: **Who was your worst boss?**

QUESTION 155

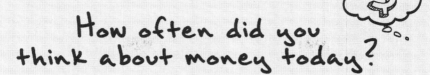

How often did you think about money today?

Date

Date

Free Space

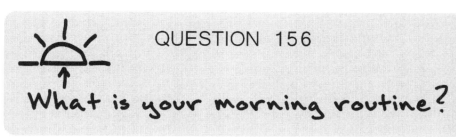

QUESTION 156

What is your morning routine?

Date

_____

_____

_____

_____

Date

Free Space

When was the last time you went to work hungover?

Date

Date

Free Space

MIND HIKE

QUESTION 158

If you were to summarize your day in a song, which song would it be?

Date

Date

Free Space

MIND HIKE

QUESTION 159

If you had to prepare a resume today, whom would you list as references?

Date
_____

_____

_____

_____

Date

Bonus Question: **Whom would you not list?**

What is one thing you can change to be more efficient?

Date
_____

_____

_____

_____

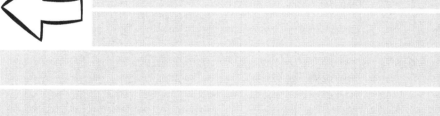

Date

Free Space

MIND HIKE

QUESTION 161

If you had to work in a different time period, which would it be?

Date

_____

_____

_____

_____

Date

Free Space

MIND HIKE

QUESTION 162

Who was the last person to take advantage of you?

Date

_____

Date

Bonus Question: That you took advantage of?

What is the most inappropriate thing that you have done at work?

Date
_____

_____

_____

_____

Date

Free Space

MIND HIKE

QUESTION 164

If you needed advice on a personal issue, which of your co-workers would you go to?

Date

Date

Free Space

MIND HIKE

Who sends the most annoying emails?

Date
_____

_____

_____

_____

Date

Free Space

QUESTION 166

When do you feel most powerful?

Date

_____

_____

_____

_____

Date

Free Space

MIND HIKE

QUESTION 167

What was the last project you avoided?

Date

_____

Date

Free Space

MIND HIKE

QUESTION 168

Which co-worker would go farthest on a reality show?

→ Date
_____

← Date

Bonus Question: In a zombie apocalypse?

MIND HIKE

QUESTION 169

What do you do when you need to escape?

Date
_____

_____

_____

_____

Date

Free Space

MIND HIKE

When was the last time
you had to apologize?

Date

Date

Bonus Question: Was it genuine?

MIND HIKE

QUESTION 171

Whom do you trust the most at your company?

Date

Date

Bonus Question: **The least?**

MIND HIKE

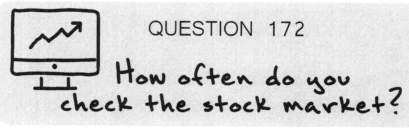

QUESTION 172

How often do you check the stock market?

Date

Date

Free Space

QUESTION 173

When was the last
time you "phoned it in"?

Date

_____

_____

_____

_____

Date

Bonus Question: Went above and
beyond?

MIND HIKE

QUESTION 174

If you lost everything, who would still be standing next to you?

Date
_____

Date

Bonus Question: **Who would leave?**

QUESTION 175

What has best prepared you for the work you do right now?

Date

Date

Bonus Question: What additional training could help you?

MIND HIKE

"Even if you are on the right track, you'll get run over if you just sit there." Will Rogers

GUIDEPOST #2: Halfway! (Halfway through the first leg of the journey, or halfway through the final leg or whichever point you find yourself on your own journey). Great job. Maybe you didn't think you would make it this far? Or, once again, maybe you skipped ahead and just found yourself at Guidepost #2? That's cool too.

TASK: Laughter is the best medicine. Draw something below that will literally make you LOL.

QUESTION 176

If you had to send one person
to live on a distant planet, who would it be?

Date

Date

Free Space

QUESTION 177

What is the best recommendation you have recently received?

Date

Date

Free Space

MIND HIKE

QUESTION 178

How are you best able
to express yourself?

Date

Date

Free Space

QUESTION 179

Who challenges you to be a better person?

Date _____

_____

_____

_____

_____

Date _____

Bonus Question: **Who do you challenge to be a better person?**

QUESTION 180

If you could block one phone number without consequence, whose would it be?

Date

Date

Bonus Question: Who is currently blocked on your phone?

MIND HIKE

QUESTION 181

What was the last risk that you took?

Date

Date

Free Space

QUESTION 182

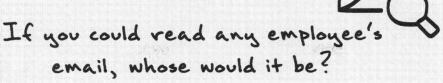

If you could read any employee's email, whose would it be?

Date

Date

Bonus Question: **Why?**

QUESTION 183

Clock is running out.
Who will shoot
the final shot?

Date
_____

_____

_____

_____

_____

Date

Bonus Question: **What if it can't be
you?**

QUESTION 184

What is the last nice thing that you did?

Date

_____

_____

_____

_____

Date

Bonus Question: **Mean thing?**

MIND HIKE

What advice do you have for your 18 year old self?

Date

Date

Free Space

MIND HIKE

QUESTION 186

If you had one year to live, how would you spend it?

Date
_____

Date

Bonus Question: 10 years?

QUESTION 187

If you were to start a blog or a podcast, what would the topic be?

Date

Date

Free Space

QUESTION 188

How transparent is your company when it comes to finances?

→ Date
_____

_____

_____

_____

← Date

Free Space

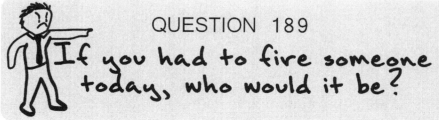

QUESTION 189

If you had to fire someone today, who would it be?

Date
_____

_____

_____

_____

Date

Free Space

QUESTION 190

What was the last impractical proposal that you had to deal with?

Date
_____

_____

_____

_____

Date

Free Space

MIND HIKE

QUESTION 191

How can your company better use its employees to the best of their abilities?

→ Date
_____

← Date

Free Space

MIND HIKE

QUESTION 192

What is your biggest regret from this past year?

Date

Date

Free Space

MIND HIKE

QUESTION 193

What leadership skill is most important for this stage of your journey?

Date

Date

Free Space

How well are your body and soul aligned?

Date

Date

Free Space

What was the last thoughtful present you gave?

Date

Date

Bonus Question: **Received?**

QUESTION 196

How close are you to the top rung of your ladder?

Date
_____

Date

Free Space

QUESTION 197

Did you follow in your parents' footsteps or family members' footsteps?

Date

Date

Bonus Question: Would you encourage a family member to follow in your footsteps?

MIND HIKE

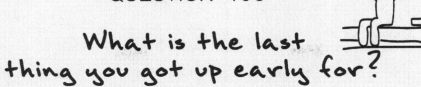

QUESTION 198

What is the last thing you got up early for?

Date
_____

Date

Free Space

Lead, follow or get out
of the way. Which are you today?

Date

Date

Free Space

MIND HIKE

QUESTION 200

How would you rate your
overall satisfaction level
this year with your company (1-10)?

Date

Date

Free Space

MIND HIKE

QUESTION 201

Who is your best
friend at work?

Date

_____

Date

Bonus Question: **Worst enemy?**

QUESTION 202

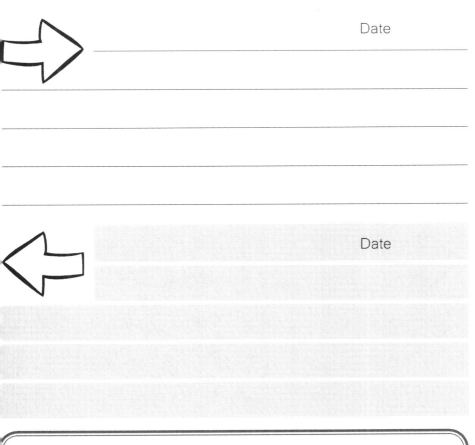

When was the last time you thought outside the box?

Date

Date

Free Space

QUESTION 203

When was the last time you showed your appreciation?

Date

Date

Free Space

MIND HIKE

QUESTION 204

How much of your identity is tied up in what you do for a living?

→ Date
_____

_____

_____

_____

← Date

Free Space

MIND HIKE

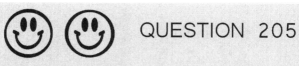

QUESTION 205

Do you end up hiring people with similar strengths to you, or different?

Date

Date

Bonus Question: How has it turned out?

MIND HIKE

QUESTION 206

How can you improve your systems?

Date
_____

Date

MIND HIKE

QUESTION 207

If you had to hire a friend, whom would it be?

Date

_____

_____

_____

_____

_____

Date

Bonus Question: How would you fire your friend?

MIND HIKE

QUESTION 208

What was the last group project you worked on?

Date

_____

Date

Bonus Question: **How well did you work together?**

QUESTION 209

If you could restart your company, what would you do differently?

Date

Date

Free Space

MIND HIKE

If you were hiring your clone, what department would they work in?

Date

Date

Free Space

MIND HIKE

QUESTION 211

Who would you want to be reincarnated as?

Date

Date

Free Space

QUESTION 212

Who is your "you have one phone call" contact?

Date
_____

Date

Bonus Question: When was the last time you called them?

MIND HIKE

QUESTION 213

When was the last
time you worked
on personal growth?

Date

Date

Free Space

MIND HIKE

What is the biggest
threat to your future?

Date

Date

Free Space

QUESTION 215

Who is the person you have the most difficulty working with?

Date

Date

Free Space

What gets you excited?

Date
_____

Date

Bonus Question: **What brings you down?**

MIND HIKE

QUESTION 217

Were you happy with the amount of effort/hours you put into your job this year?

Date
_____

Date

Bonus Question: **Will you continue this pace next year?**

QUESTION 218

What was the last purchase you made that you were excited about?

Date
_____

_____

_____

_____

Date

Bonus Question: **That you regretted?**

QUESTION 219

What would your company's official retirement present be?

Date
_____

Date

Free Space

QUESTION 220

What do you look for in a new hire?

Date

Date

Free Space

QUESTION 221

Who really knows you?

Date

_____

Date

Free Space

QUESTION 222

What is the geekiest thing you have done recently?

Date

_____

_____

_____

_____

Date

Bonus Question: Coolest?

What was your last team building exercise?

Date

Date

Free Space

MIND HIKE

QUESTION 224

"Trust but verify" – probably somebody famous and also Mike. In what ways do you buy into this idea?

Date

_____

Date

Bonus Question: When was the last time someone broke your trust?

MIND HIKE

QUESTION 225

What is one thing you could improve on?

Date

Date

Free Space

MIND HIKE

QUESTION 226

Who is your best supplier/provider/strategic partner?

Date

Date

Free Space

MIND HIKE

QUESTION 227

What inspires you?

Date

Date

Free Space

MIND HIKE

QUESTION 228

"Keep your friends close and enemies closer." What enemies are you keeping closer?

Date

_____

Date

Free Space

QUESTION 229

How much value do you place on industry recognition or awards?

Date

Date

Free Space

MIND HIKE

QUESTION 230

When was the last time you discounted your work, product, or wrote off a bill?

Date

Date

Free Space

QUESTION 231

Should your company's employees have more flexibility?

Date

Date

Bonus Question: **Why or why not?**

QUESTION 232

Which of your relationships have grown the most over the past year?

Date

_____

Date

Bonus Question: **Shrunk the most?**

MIND HIKE

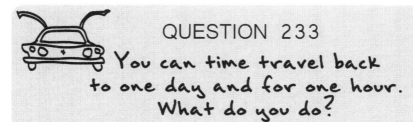

QUESTION 233

You can time travel back
to one day and for one hour.
What do you do?

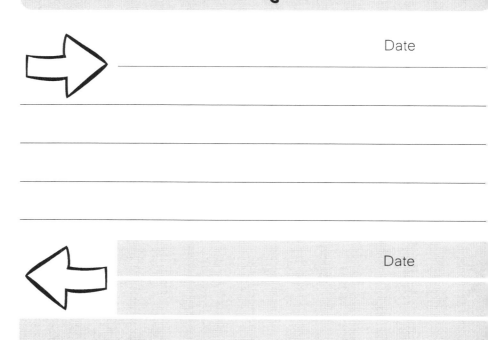

Date

Date

Bonus Question: What is your favorite
time travel movie?

QUESTION 234

What's your next adventure?

Date
_____

_____

_____

_____

Date

Free Space

QUESTION 235

Playing well with others: how important is this in your company?

Date
_____

_____

_____

_____

Date

Free Space

What has most opened up your world?

Date

Date

Free Space

QUESTION 237

What is your most important core value?

➡️ _____ Date

_____

_____

_____

⬅️ Date

Free Space

MIND HIKE

QUESTION 238

If you could have any client/customer, whom would it be?

 Date

_____

_____

_____

_____

Date

Free Space

QUESTION 239

How are you at setting boundaries?

→ Date _____

_____

_____

_____

_____

← Date

Free Space

MIND HIKE

QUESTION 240

When was the last time you got together with an old work friend?

Date

Date

Free Space

MIND HIKE

QUESTION 241

How often does your health impact your day?

Date

Date

Free Space

MIND HIKE

QUESTION 242

What is the best business decision you made this week?

Date
_____

Date

Bonus Question: **This year?**

QUESTION 243

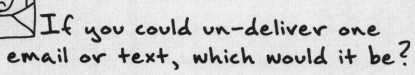

If you could un-deliver one email or text, which would it be?

Date
_____

_____

_____

_____

Date

Free Space

QUESTION 244

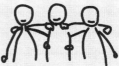

How important is it to continue working with the same core people?

Date

Date

Free Space

MIND HIKE

QUESTION 245

There's a fire at the office. What is the one thing that you grab on your way out?

→ Date
_____

_____

_____

_____

← Date

Tip: It can't be a person or a pet.

MIND HIKE

QUESTION 246

When was the last time you stepped out of your comfort zone?

Date

Date

Free Space

MIND HIKE

QUESTION 247

What are you most looking forward to?

Date
_____

Date

Bonus Question: **Least looking forward to?**

MIND HIKE

QUESTION 248

What is one small thing
you can change to
make your work day better?

Date

Date

Free Space

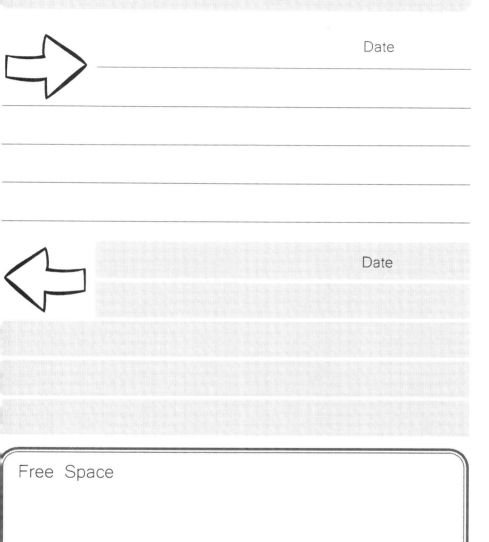

MIND HIKE

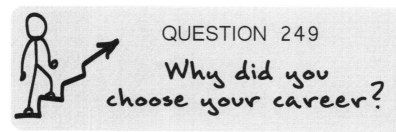

QUESTION 249

Why did you choose your career?

Date

Date

Bonus Question: **Why do you stay in it?**

QUESTION 250

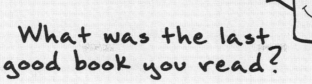

What was the last good book you read?

Date
_____

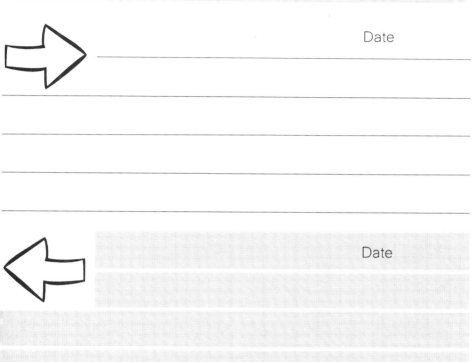

Date

Bonus Question: **Bad book?**

QUESTION 251

"Life is about the little things."
What are the little things in your life?

Date

Date

Free Space

MIND HIKE

QUESTION 252

What's your most destructive habit?

→ Date
_____

← Date

Bonus Question: **Most productive?**

QUESTION 253

What was the last goal that you set for yourself?

Date

Date

Bonus Question: Did you accomplish it? Why/why not?

QUESTION 254

Are you good at budgeting?

→ Date

_____

_____

_____

_____

← Date

Free Space

When was the last time
you received positive feedback?

Date

Date

Free Space

QUESTION 256

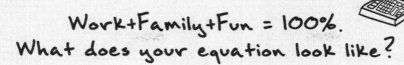

Work+Family+Fun = 100%.
What does your equation look like?

Date

Date

Free Space

QUESTION 257

When was the last time you were disappointed with a co-worker's work or behavior?

Date

Date

Free Space

MIND HIKE

QUESTION 258

When was the last time you were afraid?

Date
_____

Date

Free Space

MIND HIKE

What is(was) the most important goal today?

Date

Date

Free Space

MIND HIKE

QUESTION 260

Where will your next vacation be?

→ Date
_____

_____

_____

_____

← Date

Bonus Question: **Where was your last?**

MIND HIKE

QUESTION 261

What's the best conversation you've had recently?

Date
_____

Date

Bonus Question: **Worst?**

MIND HIKE

QUESTION 262

What has been the most
pivotal point in your career so far?

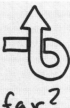

Date

Date

Free Space

MIND HIKE

QUESTION 263

What characteristic do you most value in your co-workers?

Date

_____

Date

Bonus Question: **How many have it?**

QUESTION 264

What are your guilty pleasures?

Date

Date

Free Space

QUESTION 265

What would you do
if you were given a one-month
sabbatical from work?

→   Date

←   Date

Bonus Question: **One year?**

QUESTION 266

What's your current obsession?

Date

Date

Free Space

QUESTION 267

How do you recover
from a bad day?

Date
_____

_____

_____

_____

_____

Date

Bonus Question: What caused your most
recent bad day?

MIND HIKE

QUESTION 268

How will your company be different in five years?

Date

Date

Bonus Question: **What won't ever change?**

MIND HIKE

QUESTION 269

Where is your
happy place?

Date

_____

_____

_____

_____

Date

Free Space

QUESTION 270

How long do you plan
to continue in your current role?

Date

_____

Date

Bonus Question: What will you do
after?

QUESTION 271

Who is your biggest competition right now?

→ Date
_____

_____

_____

_____

← Date

Free Space

QUESTION 272

What was your company's biggest success this year?

Date

Date

Bonus Question: Failure?

QUESTION 273

What are your 3 superpowers?

Date
_____

_____

_____

_____

Date

Free Space

QUESTION 274

What aspect of your company are you most proud of?

Date
_____

Date

Bonus Question: **Least proud?**

QUESTION 275

What was your last splurge?

Date

Date

Free Space

MIND HIKE

"Believe you can and you're halfway there." — President Theodore Roosevelt

GUIDEPOST #3: You've made it so far! Look at you, setting a goal and working so hard to meet it. You've made so much progress. You got this, dude. Keep it up.

Let's take a look behind us to appreciate how far you have come on this journey.

TASK: If this is the first leg of the journey, go back and highlight/star/asterisk 5 questions that you think will change the most when you answer them a second time. If this is the second leg of the journey, go back and highlight/star/asterisk 5 questions that changed the most when you answered them a second time.

QUESTION 276

What did you want to be when you grew up?

Date

Date

Bonus Question: What do you want to be now?

MIND HIKE

QUESTION 277

How can you be more intentional about your goals?

Date

Date

Free Space

MIND HIKE

QUESTION 278

Who is the last client/ customer you lost?

Date
_____

_____

_____

_____

Date

Bonus Question: **Why did you lose them?**

QUESTION 279

What is one thing you are grateful for?

Date

Date

Free Space

MIND HIKE

QUESTION 280

In what ways has your growth been intentional?

Date
_____

_____

_____

_____

Date

Bonus Question: Been based on the whims of fate?

MIND HIKE

QUESTION 281

When you woke up this morning, how did you feel about starting your day?

Date

Date

Free Space

MIND HIKE

QUESTION 282

If you could give a raise to only one employee, who would it be?

Date

Date

Free Space

MIND HIKE

QUESTION 283

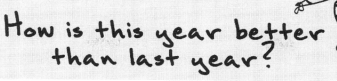

How is this year better than last year?

Date
_____

_____

_____

_____

Date

Bonus Question: **Worse?**

QUESTION 284

When was the last time you laughed out loud at work?

Date

Date

Free Space

QUESTION 285

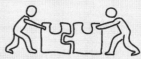

If your company had to merge with another company, which company would you choose?

Date

Date

Bonus Question: If you had to sell to another company, which company?

MIND HIKE

QUESTION 286

What was your biggest challenge today?

Date
_____

Date

Free Space

MIND HIKE

What have you done to create happiness today?

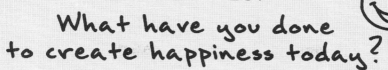

Date
_____

_____

_____

_____

Date

> "Happiness is created, not found" — Mike and the Internet

MIND HIKE

QUESTION 288

What is your biggest pet peeve?

Date

Date

Free Space

QUESTION 289

Who was the last person
you forgot having met before?

Date
_____

_____

_____

_____

Date

Bonus Question: Who was the last
person to forget your name?

MIND HIKE

QUESTION 290

What is the right way to terminate someone?

Date

Date

Free Space

MIND HIKE

QUESTION 291

If you had to acquire a company, what one would you choose?

Date

Date

Free Space

MIND HIKE

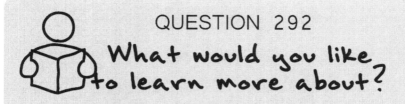

What would you like to learn more about?

Date

Date

Bonus Question: What is the first step you would take?

QUESTION 293

What was the last good business lunch/dinner you attended?

Date

Date

Bonus Question: **Most awkward?**

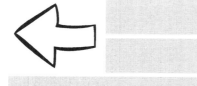

QUESTION 294

When was the last time you felt jaded?

→ Date
_____

_____

_____

_____

← Date

Tip: Jaded means tired, bored or lacking enthusiasm, typically after having had too much of something.

QUESTION 295

How can you make your company pandemic-proof?

Date
_____

_____

_____

_____

Date

Free Space

MIND HIKE

Who was the last new person you met?

Date

Date

Free Space

MIND HIKE

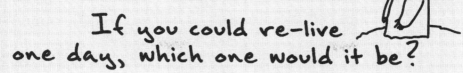

QUESTION 297

If you could re-live one day, which one would it be?

Date
_____

_____

_____

_____

_____

Date
_____

_____

_____

_____

_____

Free Space

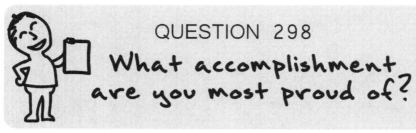

QUESTION 298

What accomplishment are you most proud of?

Date

Date

Free Space

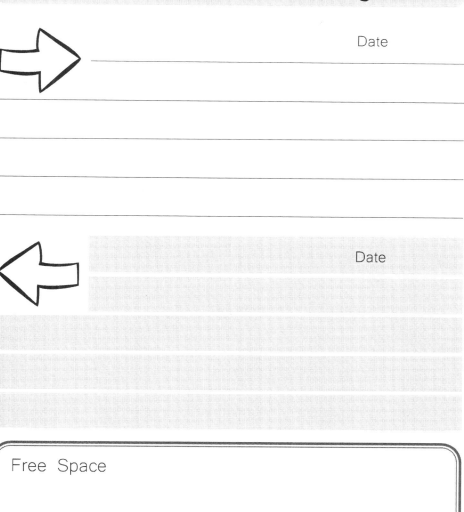

QUESTION 299

When was the last time someone doubted you?

→ Date
_____

← Date

Free Space

QUESTION 300

What is your one sentence resume?

Date

_____

_____

_____

_____

Date

Bonus Question: How old is your last resume?

MIND HIKE

QUESTION 301

What weighs most heavy on your heart right now?

Date

Date

Free Space

MIND HIKE

QUESTION 302

If you had to quit your job, where would you work?

Date

Date

Free Space

What's the best piece of advice you have received?

Date _____

Date _____

"Don't be an idiot. Changed my life." -Dwight K. Schrute

MIND HIKE

QUESTION 304

What parts of your job are you passionate about?

Date

Date

Free Space

MIND HIKE

QUESTION 305

When was the last time you made a co-worker laugh?

 Date

_____

Date

Free Space

QUESTION 306

What was the last decision that you regretted?

Date

Date

Free Space

QUESTION 307

What was the last phone call that you ignored?

Date

Date

Free Space

QUESTION 308

When was the last time you felt deflated?

Date

Date

Bonus Question: What happened?

MIND HIKE

QUESTION 309
Do you have an unspoken rule?

Date

Date

One of our favorites is: **"We don't want our clients/customers to hate talking to us."**

MIND HIKE

QUESTION 310

How happy were you
with your profitability/salary this year?

Date

Date

Free Space

QUESTION 311

How do you relax after a stressful day?

Date

Date

Free Space

MIND HIKE

QUESTION 312

What would you be
willing to do to
become more profitable?

Date

_____

Date

QUESTION 313

How has your management style improved this year?

Date
_____

_____

_____

_____

_____

Date

Bonus Question: How would your co-workers describe your management style?

MIND HIKE

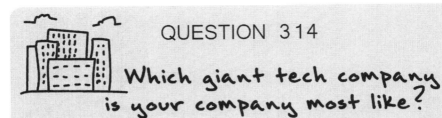

QUESTION 314

Which giant tech company is your company most like?

Date

Date

Bonus Question: Which do you want to be like?

MIND HIKE

QUESTION 315

Who would be your perfect business partner?

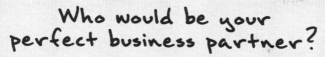

Date

Date

Free Space

MIND HIKE

QUESTION 316

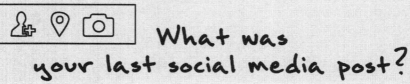

What was your last social media post?

Date

Date

Free Space

QUESTION 317

Who are your business idols?

 Date

Date

Free Space

QUESTION 318

What was the biggest challenge your company has faced this year?

Date

Date

Bonus Question: How did you handle it?

MIND HIKE

QUESTION 319

If your time was up today, what would your legacy be?

Date

Date

Free Space

QUESTION 320

What was the last thing you did for yourself?

Date

Date

Free Space

MIND HIKE

QUESTION 321

What book do you like to give as a present?

Date

Date

Free Space

QUESTION 322

What might seem minor to other people, but is a big deal to you?

→ Date

⟵ Date

Free Space

MIND HIKE

QUESTION 323

What was the last lie you told at work?

Date

Date

Free Space

What is one thing you are doing better this year than last?

Date

Date

Free Space

QUESTION 325

Who is the one that got away?

Date

Date

Bonus Question: **Why?**

MIND HIKE

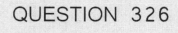

QUESTION 326

Where do you see yourself in 10 years?

Date
_____

_____

_____

_____

Date

Free Space

MIND HIKE

QUESTION 327

What was the last decision that you made on principle?

Date

Date

Free Space

MIND HIKE

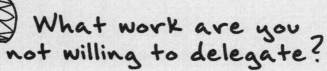

QUESTION 328

What work are you not willing to delegate?

Date
_____

_____

_____

_____

Date

Free Space

MIND HIKE

QUESTION 329

Are you on the right path?

Date

Date

Bonus Question: Why/why not?

MIND HIKE

What is the single best thing that you contribute to your company?

Date

_____

_____

_____

_____

Date

Free Space

QUESTION 331

How many days off
(real days off)
did you take last year?

Date
_____

_____

_____

_____

Date

Bonus Question: **Was it the right amount?**

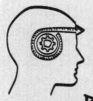

QUESTION 332

How can you be more
proactive instead of reactive?

Date

Date

Free Space

QUESTION 333

"What would you do if you weren't afraid?" - Sheryl Sandberg

Date
_____

_____

_____

_____

Date

Free Space

MIND HIKE

QUESTION 334

What cliched line would you use to describe this last year?

Date

Date

Free Space

MIND HIKE

QUESTION 335

Who is your biggest adversary?

Date
_____

_____

_____

_____

Date

Free Space

QUESTION 336

What is the last problem
that you fixed
with money?

Date

Date

"Any problem that can be fixed
with money isn't the worst problem
to have." – Elissa's Dad

QUESTION 337

What did you learn from your last failure?

Date
_____

Date

Free Space

QUESTION 338

If your business partner
(or 2nd in command)
left you tomorrow, what would you do?

Date

Date

Free Space

MIND HIKE

QUESTION 339

What is your biggest edge over your competition?

→ Date
_____

← Date

Free Space

QUESTION 340

When was the last time you had to speak up about an uncomfortable problem?

Date

Date

Free Space

MIND HIKE

QUESTION 341

Who was the last person to ask for a raise?

Date
_____

Date

Or when was the last time you asked for a raise?

MIND HIKE

When was the last time
you moved for work?

Date

Date

Free Space

MIND HIKE

QUESTION 343

How well are you keeping up with the times?

➡️ Date
_____

⬅️ Date

Free Space

QUESTION 344

When was the last time you were brave?

→ Date
_____

_____

_____

_____

_____

← Date

Free Space

What would be at the top of your do-not-do-list these days?

Date
_____

_____

_____

_____

Date

Free Space

MIND HIKE

QUESTION 346

What was the last question that you couldn't answer?

→ Date
_____

← Date

Free Space

MIND HIKE

QUESTION 347

When was the last time you had to have the last word?

Date

Date

Free Space

MIND HIKE

QUESTION 348

What is your favorite saying?

Date

_____

_____

_____

_____

Date

Free Space

MIND HIKE

QUESTION 349

When was the last time you swallowed your pride?

Date

Date

Free Space

MIND HIKE

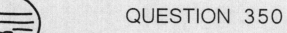

QUESTION 350

Which of your current clients/customers would give you a bad review?

→ Date
_____

_____

_____

_____

← Date

Free Space

QUESTION 351

When were you last surprised at work?

Date

_____

Date

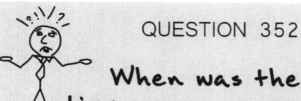

QUESTION 352

When was the last time you gave an excuse?

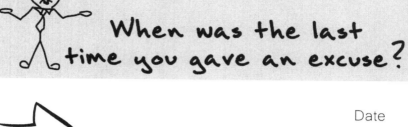

Date
_____

_____

_____

_____

_____

Date

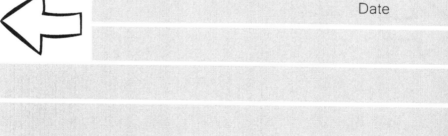

Free Space

QUESTION 353

When was the last time you were impatient?

Date
_____

Date

Free Space

QUESTION 354

What is your perfect mental health day?

Date

Date

Free Space

MIND HIKE

QUESTION 355

What is one thing
that your company
does to retain employees?

Date

_____

_____

_____

_____

Date

Free Space

MIND HIKE

When was the last time you really enjoyed the present?

Date

Date

"[man] is so anxious about the future that he does not enjoy the present." – Dalai Lama

QUESTION 357

What was the last thing that was broken that you fixed?

Date
_____

Date

Bonus Question: **That you haven't fixed?**

MIND HIKE

QUESTION 358

What was the last expensive company purchase and was it worth it?

Date

Date

"This just cost $100 for us to go here for the day, so you'd better have fun." – David's dad outside of Disney World to young David.

QUESTION 359

How difficult has it been to keep going on this journey?

Date
_____

_____

_____

_____

Date

Free Space

MIND HIKE

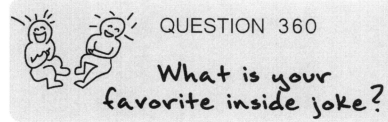

QUESTION 360

What is your favorite inside joke?

Date

Date

Free Space

QUESTION 361

You learn something new every day. What have you learned today?

Date

Date

Free Space

MIND HIKE

QUESTION 362

The average human lifespan is approximately 28,725.5 days. How are you making this day count?

Date

Date

Free Space

MIND HIKE

QUESTION 363

What are three things that you are grateful for at your company?

Date
_____

Date

Free Space

MIND HIKE

QUESTION 364

What is your favorite snack in the break room?

Date

Date

Free Space

MIND HIKE

QUESTION 365

[FILL IN THE BLANK. What question do you want to answer today?]

Date

Date

Free Space

MIND HIKE

"Sometimes the questions are complicated and the answers are simple." — Dr. Seuss

GUIDEPOST #4: You made it! We're happy to see you here. If you've made it all the way through your 365 questions (or through them twice), you've been working hard, and we salute you. Enjoy the view!

Whether this is the first leg or the final leg of your Mind Hike journey, we encourage you to spend a little time reflecting on yourself. If we weren't so cheap, we might have included a neat little mirror on this page. But instead we are asking you to do the hard work.

TASK: Create a self-portrait of how you see yourself today (below). You can use words or a collage or a paint brush or your favorite crayon.

....

....

....

....

....

....

Great Job. You have completed the first half of your Mind Hike journey. Now turn around and start again at Question 1.

You made it! You have completed your Mind Hike journey. We hope you enjoyed it!

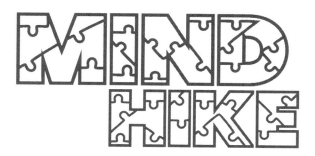

Made in the USA
Middletown, DE
05 November 2020